LONG

SHADOWS

OF

PRACTICE

LONG
SHADOWS
OF
PRACTICE

POEMS

BETH JACOBS

Homebound Publications

Ensuring that the mainstream isn't the only stream.

HOMEBOUND PUBLICATIONS

WWW.HOMEBOUNDPUBLICATIONS.COM

HOMEBOUND PUBLICATIONS IS A REGISTERED TRADEMARK OF HOMEBOUND PUBLICATIONS

© 2021 TEXT BY BETH JACOBS

Quantity sales. Special discounts are available on quantity purchases by corporations, associations, bookstores, and others. For details, contact the publisher or visit wholesalers such as Ingram or Baker & Taylor.

All Rights Reserved
Published in 2021 by Homebound Publications
Cover Design and Interior Design by Leslie M. Browning
ISBN: 9781953340122
First Edition Trade Paperback

10 9 8 7 6 5 4 3 2 1

Look for our titles in paperback, ebook, and audiobook wherever books are sold. Wholesale offerings for retailers available through Ingram. Homebound Publications and its divisions are distributed by Publisher's Group West.

Homebound Publications, is committed to ecological stewardship. We greatly value the natural environment and invest in environmental conservation. For each book purchased in our online store we plant one tree.

CONTENTS

SENSU THE BOAT MONK

Back and forth in a red wood boat
My shoulders like cords from so much rowing
The river's cool color never repeats
Its own braided currents meet and remeet

Some step in lightly though at the end
Their toes reach and wiggle for sand
Like the sniffing nose of a dog
My hand steadies their step

The light, sweet slap of the lap
Of the water hypnotizes most
The way over is long
The angle to the bank precise

The grinding wet sand
Announces our arrival
I step out to pull, the lighter
Ones easier on my back

My pant legs rolled up
But always are wet
On the final night run
I'll roll them again

So I can walk home slow and tired
Against chill evening air
The ground suddenly hard
My arms uncannily light

TETRALEMMA I

We see objects
    but they are all looking right back at us
The mind moves the spotlight of attention
    but ideas and images twirl around and fly in the dark
The tree is lace against the sky
    but the roots are grasped to the dirt's breast
A person is born and dies
    but a life keeps bobbling the turnstile
    after the subway rumbles by

THUSNESS

When it rains a fat worm of a stream advances
across the matte boredom of the driveway
bright black with silver sparkling pings of drops
The suburban forsythia becomes 45 keyboards
being played madly at cross purposes
and the thunder rolls the light off to the left
and pushes the wet smell of air to the right
as I sit with a coffee mug in an open garage
to watch the show
how it exudes itself
and only itself
with such freedom
All is awareness in uniquely receptive domains
Experience holds in the practices of letting go

HEARTWOOD

"But it is this unshakable liberation of mind that is the goal of this spiritual life, its heartwood, and its end." – Majjhima Nikaya 29: Mahasaropama Sutta: I

The gulls cry oi like New Yorkers
while the beach is all gold and cerulean
a sugar haze grazes the horizon
a lone grape sits strangely in sand
and here under the mustard twigged willow
a being in light and shade
back against strong ridges of bark
fractures the world with description
and eats the pieces like candy

What did those bald robed ones see?
They tread this same world in its younger days
but they cracked it open with minds so pure
they moved without bumping reality
they stepped without grinding dirt
they saw without unfolding the distance
they saw like touch
and touched like babies
they spoke willow

AT THE MONASTERY

A space where many people meditate
acquires a density of intention
that hovers like a blanketing fog and
makes thoughts less flammable
The clanky apparatus of making a self becomes obvious
but still folds its metallic linear arms around experience
While experience balances
like the construction worker
on a steel beam eating a sandwich
eighty stories above Times Square
Maybe the sandwich is delicious
Maybe it isn't
It's just lunchtime

REBIRTH

Before I was born a viola player died
The viola player left
the asymmetrical stretch of the neck
and the glow of the curved dark wood
how the thumb seeks the notch on the bow
and the four fingers long to fan
their bridge truss on the other side

Maybe in a shtetl, maybe on a street
maybe in a hall, maybe with candlelight
head tilt to clavicle, sharp edged smell of rosin
eyes pulled narrow by love of the notes' flow
the viola player tapped his foot softly
pulling precision over the arm crooked in a baby hold

That part I got
although I fumbled some on the follow-through
I so appreciate the richness
that tone of caramel generous bloodwarmth
how kind to play this old worn flower
how much it all matters

THE KNOLL

I'm letting myself not flee something blowing in
The sky is whiting up and gulls are crisscrossing
Waves are asserting and the air is stiff
The locust tree is warning the unprepared
but decided

Behind the air there is something to be pulled
from the sky that is beyond skill and patience
a last turquoise streak in roiling cornflower blue
A big bunch of gulls comes now
hysterical

If all the words were whitecaps and all the
pages wetness it could still work
So many ways it could work
more than the human apparatus notes or makes
but not more than the wind

OVERTURNED

Like a prisoner released
from a wrongful conviction
I drop the belief
and constriction caused
by accusation
A young mind
barraged by such unfairness
crumples
but if it doesn't break
and it is pressed
over and over by palms
of smooth hands
the message can often
still be read
The Writ of exoneration
clutched as I blink
in the sudden light
on courthouse steps
allows the innocence
of a hard-working heart
Love's slow efforts
even incarcerated
accrue connection

Both grief and grace
are rightly available
I stumble down
the marble stairs
I can hear the plural racket
of a single cicada
and see sturdy oaks
lining the town square
I've been set free
in an unknown home

TWO DEATH STORIES

Both of these tales were told to me first hand:

One, a young and healthy man who died
on a meditation cushion called a zafu
at a beautiful Zen monastery in the Southwest
during a long meditation retreat
staring at the adobe wall before him
facing the particulars of his mind or not
he sat where those particulars had an opportunity
to be perceived in a broader context and
he stopped Slowly he slumped to the side
and was gone

Two, an older man sick for a while
laid in a rented hospital bed
set on the first floor
of a white house by the ocean
a kindly and helpful man
leaving a life of service and earnest joys
so angry he cursed his beloved wife
and withdrew Stepped off the platform
into the amnesia of the
earliest years of hostility and envy

All that I do is really about training
my own end to be more like the first death
I work to face the foundational brutality
I practice dropping so I can leave awake
and taste the great matters of birth and death
while in between the wheel turns
rot breaks down organically to mulch
 something that labored to float in the sky
becomes sky

HOW TO DROP A THOUGHT

What if you could roll out smoke like dough?

Your velvet rolling pin smooths out a thin layer

a misty gray sheet

You trim it with scissors to a three-foot square

not quite transparent

You carefully lift the vapor shape

by diagonal corners

and you walk to the window

The open window looks over a valley

Mountains recede in blue dolphin jumps

You stretch your tremulous bare arms

over the chilled evening expanse

and pop open your fingers that held the vague material

and it floats

It drops to the left

then dance-ducks to the right

On the next pivot inward

you lose sight of it

Instead you hear wind

and taste mountain light

A TERRIBLE REALISM

A mourning dove is not sad
Her muted howls are her own energy
her own air pumped through
the shapes inside the being that she is

The grief I hear is mine
Her cry moves it beyond
my chest and heart
and all that is lost

And the mourning dove is not hurt
by my imputation
On yonder roof unseen
she freely emits her series of three

Still the moment of
bird breast contraction meets ear
runs clear beneath it all
uncolored by human noting

While I wrote this poem
six eggs I forgot
I was boiling
blew up in the clean kitchen

It took three explosions
for me to realize
it was not just the cat
batting things around

What a sight; splattered
shell and egg white and yellow
Sound meets ear and
rag meets floor

ALLOWANCE

The tree accepts
all weather moving through branches
updrafts and downward tugs
wet and arid breezes
air with chill or inviting warmth
The tree entertains
all the crisscrossed ellipses
of rotating orbs and lights
causing shadows to unevenly
sundial around the base
and wobble up the trunk
So also the heart
knows and feels everything
and all seasons
have already imprinted
from that first moment
of emerging
when light was so glaring
it was more blinding than darkness

HOW CHANGE HAPPENS

"Dharma gates are boundless; I vow to enter them."
[Part of traditional Zen Buddhist chant after study]

First you must Volunteer to Dissolve
Say it to yourself three times
Then
Attention's flailing resumes
like the spray of water
from the unattended hose
as it writhes in the grass

You writhe also
under the guise of
deadlines, chest pains, blame and
hasty attachments
You repeat the incantation
now with a putrid streak of doubt
and you don't know to what
you have opened the door
or that it's ajar

You're jarred; you brought it on

and it's such a cold fog

with such strong saturation

When you said dissolve

you were picturing sugar

not this situation

Watch the gray shapes

take focus in the mist

as the mouth of new things opens

(PREPOSITION) SPACE

She pulls the scissors from the pocket of her puffy suit
and slashes the tether to the space module
and allows herself to float off
She carries a jagged saw up into the tree
and sits on the outermost twig
while the blade chews into the wood
She foregoes all prepositions
allowing it all to match up
any which way

The release is lightness that sits heavy in the chest
The view of blindness is crushing
and the sorrow of pure solitude is chronic
Off she flies singing impossible truth
while the hawk pumps against icy air
while the dense body registers every flutter

DUST COLLECTS SHADOWS

In honor of Amanda Baggs

Dust collects shadows

Shadows define edges

Edges allow difference

Difference evokes evaluation

Evaluation is confusing

Confusion evolves into delusion

Delusions create worlds

Worlds float lightly

Lightness gives heart

Heart is seen in still things

Still things collect dust

INCENSE SMOKE SAMADHI

If you could taste
the incense smoke's
ribbon variations
as they hit you in the air
you would be enlightened

Incense ribbon is only air
where the current
is announced
The current is only the sum
of all prevailing forces
glacier slow and subcapillary
ancient and live
in front and behind
The soft grayblue swirl
of instant tendril animation
is only a kiss on your face
that makes your eyes water

In a quiet moment
if you move with it
and your thoughts
curl away with it

and your whole being
doubles back
with a jellyfish style
convulsion and propulsion
because of it
then you are enlightened

A LOCAL SELF

if you take the express train
you miss the stop
but the town is still there
you will end up back
in its familiar orb
with no reason for
its feeling of being known
you've been up and down the line
you didn't pick your home
but somewhere in the swarm
or matrix or wet tissue
of the world
is the hot spot
felt zone of interaction
and the bruised domain
of tenderness
that indicate your own station
when the tracks cross there
you have a lever
in the conductor's car
the course can deviate
or derail or rotate in space
and still your hub
hugs every other

FELT

just
learn and yearn and wish
for this purpose
let this
tragic and impossible
and flawed thing
happen
just
get out of the way
remove monuments
allow light
to move
like a river
branching out
to a blinding sea

INTERPERSONAL

The sinkhole between us
is always its whole self
growing and reaching
like our comical arms
extended to each other
over it and stretching
like the pink color of
cat tongues, pencil erasers
and pigeon feet
Our elasticity and complicity
bind us in live cities
and on the edge
the pull and push and blindness
in constant negotiation
and failing diplomacy
have their say
but never sway the effort
The gulf is enormous
the riveted longing bigger

SO STICKY

The overblown self is so sticky
that shaking it off
is like you dip your fingers in oil
and clean the floor of the barbershop
without a broom
Greed is so buoyant
that losing it
is like you submerge a ping pong ball
in a bucket of water
and you can touch it only
with the sharpened point of a pencil
Insight is so fleeting
that preserving it
is like you carry water
over boulders
in a baking tray
Fear is so potent
that crushing it
is like you stack feathers
on a subway track
 between trains
The Dharma is so radial
that this is all irrelevant
and fiercely true and beautiful
like starlight
on a squirrel's tail

TETRALEMMA II

We walk together knee-deep in the thick snow
    and every flake bears a fractal world
No it's actually all cool bleached flour
    and pattern is visible in our swirling wake
No it's actually swimming not wading
    and we're in over our heads in the silken stir of it
No we're actually flour too
    and every motion mixes beyond the merger

THE FORM OF IT

In a mysterious blot
consciousness coheres
inside of a body
and after the body
the glue of longing
bundles a ghost

With fewer sticky wishes
the mist moves more freely
(but desire is never stifled
only unlocked
when preference loosens
and allowance opens)

With less density of holding
old and flowing knowing
drifts more openly
This is helpful
to those currently embodied
We are given little steers
and invisible course corrections
so we hit unseen borders
with less force
and trample fewer
subtle gardens

OAK

Old oaks
old bench
worn shoes
no poem is old
none is young
but all stay new

Old heart
knows sorrow and wind
well as the wrinkled oak branch
in its frozen convolution
of rightly placed
salvation

CLINGING TO EXISTENCE

Grief is the backlight of
love silhouetted and gnarly
It is good to be stupidly alive
even if distracted
through the whole show
Right now I'd rather see
and smell and crunch leaves
than know truth
Black branches are a squint
away from the dark sky and
the beating light of a plane
impossibly holds
a hundred warm bodies

FATHER'S DAY

On Father's Day
my own brutal parent dead several years
I watch my husband spend two hours
to attach his daughter's license plate to her car
Sweating muttering
bins of screws
orange extension cord
unraveled to the garage
She offers him water and coy audience
I want to scream or do dishes or eat chips
Later I cannot stop the recycling of experience
with variation
sage relief I missed and vengeance I deserve
when I spot the thread of realization and wrap it around a finger
It doesn't bear my weight but it doesn't break
I tug and feel it cut into my skin and tug some more
The dishes are clean and the chips gone
and perspective pivots:
First stupidity doesn't belie sympathy
All the dumb sources of pain root deep
Second it must run its course
Dams just flood the banks
Third right now there is something in front of my face
needing attention
Realtime raindrops ping leaves
and the muse hummingbird visits the pine tree

TERROR

Come in my friend
I like you best undressed
but this new costume
becomes you become it
and it fits

Come in my friend
take a long draught of a kiss
over the abyss
and don't tip forward or in
but taste where we mix

Come in my friend
you don't need to lurk
behind the doorjamb like Boo Radley
you're pale from hiding
and the light dissolves your habit

Come on in
you're everpresent anyway and diffuse
and we will share this wooden space
since you're so tired and just and fair
take a chair

APERTURE AFTER STRUCTURE

It feels urgent of course
before the apocalypse
but after you've become old
and put in your time studying the masters
your task is to wait

The gusts of wind
preceded by stampedes of leaf cartwheels
sucked across the grass
will invisibly inform
those sitting on park benches
only if you've made a thousand children's lunches
or put in continents behind the wheel
delivering what's necessary
or made books or money or collections or messes
or order or images or beds or love

Especially if you found ways to make love happen
you can rest in a park
See the solemn clouds proceed north
regal and front lit
See the gulls before them disappear when they turn
all of the densities fluctuating
like the life you sink into more and more
as it softly disperses

NOT THE POEM I MEANT
TO WRITE FOR JANE

Because the poet picked a rock to sit on
in the woods
with a footrest of a yellow jacket nest
and the karma ripened
just then
it seems very obvious
about cause and unexpected effect
as eighteen electric awakenings
and a lip the size of Indiana
show the poet
that a new poem has taken over
gobbling up every idea in its tornado swarm
blowing through the path and the background
insisting on vacuuming me up into it

UNWINDING

The dharma default has set in
I'm more settled and
sinking feelings are no longer alarming
Ropes and pulleys
that conveyed me down the well
have dissolved
I've lost touch
with the point of origination

Imagination and the tangible
are reconciling
The forward view
is from the bottom of a funnel
and the range of possibility
broadens in each moment

There was a time
when sensations such as these
were successfully warded off
coated and cultured
cast back or clipped

I'm not saying I boldened
or chose it but maybe
just roamed over
slow-heaving mossy carpets
in unseen old marshes
allowing the weight of each step

RE'MEMBER

Put those limbs back together
over and over although they were
brutally and bloodily hacked
in the wars of the soul
magically like rewinding film
they will reattach
and the red blood
will flow backwards
and disappear in the crack

Remember the present
put it back together
that warm snap of association
can happen for now
as well as for history
the more often the present is renewed
the deeper it runs
the thinner the cracks
in its animated cohesion

Apply once again
for entrance to the club
Every time you knock on the door
with your knuckles

against grained wood
 you are readmitted
and being a member again
reminds your relief
Right now you are home

ZAZEN TODAY

"Don't ever think you can sit zazen. That's a big mistake. Zazen sits zazen."
–Suzuki Roshi quoted by Zenkei Blanche Hartman in *Seeds for a Boundless Life*

I hear the crackle of associations
splintering exponentially into emptiness
I feel awareness' pinprick
touch on various automatic processes of mind
that occur reflexively
concurrently and spontaneously
Here is Silent Night running
in the background for ten minutes
Here is a fantasy that blooms and loops
crouched to resume
And a blob of thought
not yet sharpened into scissored words
Here is the Describer as she scrambles
for a leg up over a black marble wall
always a slow backward slide down
And here is grief awaiting, brewing
biding its luxurious time
knowing it has already won

ELEVATORS

The beauty
of the staggering 200 meter
gray and green streaked
rough rock wall before you
is not that you are so
tiny relative to it but
that scale dissolves

The holiness
of Wind Cave tunnels
where the Oglala Lakota
place their creation event
is not the surface of
glittering crust and box shaped lace
but the unseen porousness
that makes the body recall
being able to breathe
under water

The hardship
of consciousness is not
from touching upon pain and shame

and awareness of death but
from its own misplacement of itself
from experiencing a lost mind
looking for home
with the wrong map

THE FIVE RANKS

A big horizon
always meets the mind
dome joins dome
but the eyes don't abide
they dart and scan
while each wave by the shore
with its own herd of foam
intones a broken note

The lines of waves
left in wet sand
are sketches of mountain ranges
constantly building
by receding
at the base

I tore some lines
from a beautiful book
and pasted them in my chest
so the ancestors
could infuse me
while I bleed and breathe
and the letters break up
inside me like seeds

For seeds inside dirt
orientation is natural
and every little particle
in every direction
whispers some truth

Where the horizon lies
is a lie about edges
Where it imagines a meeting
is salvation and fruit

WHEN THERE IS NO TIME FOR THE POEMS

First the levees broke
and also many necks
and then a dominos effect
Barriers of repression and disavowal
cracking dissolving flooding
in chunks of concrete and awareness
The surge carries bits
of every forgotten detail and item
and every corrupted
moment of connection
All returned and blowing right by
to remind and dismantle mind
all at the same time
If there isn't a thing or two
to grab in the rush
and craft into a message
then all hope is lost

THE REDS

There were so many reds
and so potent
in the peonies in sunlight
that I got knocked back
with third degree red blindness
and only the capacity to note
I circled back over and over
and stayed overcome by the reds
each hue its own
cry of red
punch of red
twang of red
slaying by red
How weak to gossip
of a color
when I want to drown in it
How wrong to refer
when I prefer to submerge
I took pictures
I snatched comparatives
and still the seventeen pulses
of red remain

There were so many moving reds

living and dying before me

living and dying with them

in each instant

bathed in thrust

thrust in light

so red

the flowers turned transparent

and the reds took off

smearing worlds and retinas

and bringing only that quality

to everything

WORDLESS

Inhale this one : reminiscent

Feel it saturate your already shiny wet lobes

Bat this away : again

While you are there, please crush this

with the palm of your hand or your heel

but be careful for thorns : needy

drop : dizzy

splat : nausea

bounce : peripheral until it rolls into the wall and returns

Keep going until you are alone and silent

Keep going until language abandons you

Keep going

No matter how far back you step

you need a word for infinity

I HATE POEMS ABOUT POEMS

The poem is so noisy
the words richocet
against my skull
jangle on the way down
moan loudly in a heap
The lines demand me
They bloom conscious
and bleed forward
on the paper
Letters march like parades
for dictators and insist
I salute and I do
for they rule
and for my obeisance reward me
with quiet

THE SCRIBE

My back is a question mark bent from straining
to aid my eyes which are dim from straining
for the text I copy which is dense from straining
for the truth

In this globe of golden candlelight
my wooden stool and tilted desk board
meet the pelvic and elbow angles leaning
into my work

I ache for each word I carefully carry
and lay in its place with its weighty draped body
like the companions already waiting
on the page

I dip for more ink with fingers like twigs
The parchment sucks color and I give it a drink
as to a kitten with closed eyes taking a drop of milk
on her tongue

I'm a way station for words and I work from the corner
There is only portage as words suffer no owner
A letter's fine arch defines the domain
of a scribe

MEDITATING IN VOLCANOES

for Tricia

Stay still when big orange embers and black ashes fall
to develop a skill that is hard-earned and useful
because if you're waiting to see if your son is alive
or just if your ticket will be called
it's the same because you don't know
in your human mind
though it's frustrating to recall
that you've already been through the future
and just can't find it now

Don't hold to future visions
but drop them like the hot coals they are
and try to find the right quiet thing to repeat
just one thing to do the same every day
and especially if it makes openings inside
and especially if it has a tiny cleanse feel
or a fizzure in something crusty
or a miniscule drift or disappearance
behind the eyes

The quick-of-the-moment stillness freezes even lava
that you know is flowing towards you
and you can live just for that instant
when the words are waiting outside the door
with their tickets to the show
in the fine white powder of volcano dust

TETRALEMMA III

Once you visualize the Bodhisattva exponential explosion
  you have nothing to say
If you have some clear sense of how many things are impacting your state
  you have no choices left to make
If your body drops into its own outline with enough density
  you have nowhere to go
If you see how lovingly the soft blues revolve to the horizon
  you have nothing left to feel

DELUSIONS

I look at my son and cry

Why won't you take up arms against your illness?

He looks at me and replies

Who are you to tell me what gods to worship?

I despair of his suffering

fears of things unseen

the deforming waves of pain

Then I think of the twinkling indigo gods

looking at me and feeling the same

Why traipse after rickety thought and order?

Why do you pull that blanket up over your head?

It's warm outside and

the soft lights diffuse beauty

THE POINT OF VIEW

only the lunatic remembers
that our common first act
is to burst forth
into air from between
two curtains of flesh

only the mad people feel
the pulse of hatred
and the repellant pushback
inside very morsel of
human connection

only the ill are free
of the clear wall
so icy and impenetrable
that the molten heart
can never melt it

only the unwell know
what's in the well
while teary eyes can't swim
in the inky depths

MY RELATIONSHIP WITH GRAVITY

Gravity and I have come to terms with each other
at a lingering lunch anchoring the flotation of fate
He complained that I load too much per volume
having been that very serious child and getting it
that he starts with the grave and not the cradle
Yet gravity's compassion never abandoned
my compression tendency until recently
Gravity lost that firm hold in the chair
and sweet release in travelling air
shown in blown leaves and seeds
I loved gravity and felt betrayed
in the spasm of gut smacked loss
and levitations of dread impact
How tough are gravity abetted
plunges against tender bodies
Gravity and I kissed quickly
before we left and pierced
each other's vacant eyes
I took the coatcheck stub
to pick up disorientation
and faith in emptiness
where you can't fall
without down and
you can't drown
without

up

IT'S THERE

The body is taught
to hide a feeling
in endless disguises
and black shadows
Open-faced love
gone rogue and vague
in a glaucoma of desire
wonders and wanders
in bad spaces
and vacant cavities
Seekers track
the clues on the trail
like the faint scent
of generosity
On the edge
of a barely recalled
angle of a cheekbone
a smarting hint
breaks through
the bruised pebble
lodged in the chest
gray with veins of glitter
When that geode dissolves
its prism laid open
the light moans and goes

GOOD AT JOY

For Doralee

Being good at joy
isn't waterwheels
but an elegant fingered allowance
of the tiny undergeyser of it
between worlds
and a way eyes flutter
as the molecules bounce
on the top of the fountain
To be comfortable
with seepage and leaks
and not jump sponges
on what's coming next
Somehow to remember
to comb through the hair of air
before you've past the last
 invisible tendril of it

ATTUNED TO TINY

My cousin's Japanese wife
spoke little English
and me, no Japanese
Her intuitive translation
was flawless
and she bought me a picture
A little potato-shaped monk
with two littler potato people
just like me and my children
a watercolor strip of river
orange crawfish and funny spirals
She explained the calligraphy poem
Something like Are you aware?
Are you seeing?
So many details
before you, little details
Oh no she laughed it's not scolding
Just, Are you seeing?
I didn't half understand
but I totally did and didn't
at the same time

Now moments come forward
and if they aren't shot up
with my vision
of what they should be
the little details come to me
The ring that the mug left
on the black stove top
is not an O but a Q
Wind's democracy of motion
and the economy of dew
A feather-light thud
when an inch of incense ash
burns down and tumbles

Thank you for the print Chizuko
It's hanging where my eyes open
from sleep and see
Many saviors of my overwrought soul
unblinded me

THE BASEMENT OF FAITH

Like a cartoon character
falling through the branches
bouncing and oofing and refolding
at the waist with every blow
I have been there
as every floor of Faith Tower
collapsed in heaps of dust
and rebar-ripped rubble
and infinite crumble
no landing possible
Empirical certainty
abandons regularly
and it's really just sap
and being a sap
and how sticky sweet stuff
oozes where pine
branches snap

AIR CARRIES

The weight of a banana peel holds in this breeze
but not paper; hold only what you need and need to
There is nothing I need to know here
Every day I live with what I said
I couldn't live with yesterday
And it keeps stripping down my mind
steps out of silly silky slips with thoughts' bare feet
on wood floors and I wouldn't do more
if I could for the wind bears enough
like the words; some fluff and some substantive
some flutter and some tumble but all go
where the forces blow and converge and verify
the heart's true weight

PANDEMIC JOURNAL

We write to document
what is unbelievable to our own selves
in the current moment's impact
to break up our stunned visions
and grind them down like
glass to a new lens constantly
We write to slow the kaleidoscope's roll
of complexity and bits of bright color
in wedges of symmetry
We write to break down
the unbearable fascination
that won't quit when we feel
how precious it all is
and how little control we own
how very little we own
We are writing because
what we call prehistory
is only a failure of imagination
in one direction
and what we call future
is only a conglomeration
of emotion turned vivid under pressure
Extreme wish and dread
The blank white made of every color
even ones we never named

WHEN THE CROWS YELL AT YOU

Don't let them scare you off. Or do.
Caw back with all your heart. Or lose
your way in the ruckus. They're
raucous; their caucus is stirring it up.
They own the place. They're tough.
Their sheen shines. Their force finds
its way through the oak grove.
Leaves' nubby green thumbs meet
crows' suddenly-fingered flight.
Smooth black against any texture
wins. Crows' caws baptize away
sins. The crow is form in flight.
Its path a splash of black light.

CULTIVATING LIGHT

The earthly garden needs light
The metagarden of light needs even brighter things
Waft it through with open space to bloom
Crystal it down with objects to fall upon
Water light with clear cohesion and potency
It is not enough to pesticide the crawling dark invaders
The hot creative source requires our love and sacrifice

THE MISSIONARY BAPTIST
AND THE BODHISATTVA

do the exact same thing
because it usually boils down
to lugging heavy sacks
and often groceries
and salvation is the focus
and concrete care the means
The ground of it all
has so many names
it seems fancy to discuss
our prejudice in setting it up
but shouting Jesus
brings its own carriage
and I wish I could cook like Lisa
and pray like Rebecca
My bag of notebooks
and juice boxes lands right here
where all the lucid ancestors
give the live body the power
to tote the load I know
while this specific gallon of blood
in this particular network flows

LET LOVE EXPLODE

let love explode
although you know
you've grown enough
and lost so much

the years have ripped
big parts of you
we've all tried to grip
to sand and fresh wind

we've spoken the flat
vowels of grief
felt the outcast
peer back in

the dropper is poised
with jet black ink
over a glass bowl of water
in the sunlit kitchen

squeeze the dropper
and see black blossom
over and over
although you know

A SPRING DAY IN THE PANDEMIC

A photographer takes pictures of a mother
with her newborn at the beach
but can only zoom in with the long lens
To be born in a pandemic
the soul must have tap dancing feet
Every step back congratulates
the new frame naively
Like every day after sickness feels recovered
Like every day not dead feels alive
and still perspective goes on wryly growing
Another young mother walks by
who can text with one hand
and push the stroller with the other
The oblivious bunny eats grass
and innocence continuously refills itself
as it slips through war's vast ravine
The hinted taste of spring air
comes in every pore
The unimaginable blooms
beside a white crocus

INVISIBLE CURRENTS

mysterious alignments and accordances
and accordions of course

mustard colored filter
on autumn's daring light

scaleless tininess
just the granular minifeel of truth

infinite radial bowtie convergence
merge emerge emergent intersections

come on down and be in it
put on socks if your feet are cold

"TO THOSE WHO STUDY THE MYSTERY"
from the poem *Sandokai* by Sekito Kisen

A twist of smoke draws a squint from us all
But no one saw the same gray ribbon
    We huddle around fire in a trance
    Inside is a silent gray sea we can sense
We swim together in a silent sea
And cast language nets over mystery
    Each word we use carries a net
    Or bears a kite tail that turns and flips in the wind
The common wind carries separate seeds
We meet where we touch shared earth
    The earth is our witness
    The elements our difference
Our differences are total
We all speak sangha as a second family
    We bring shards of family to the group
    And heaps of gooey longing too
We share longing and divide resources
We make silence together and combine into chords
    We shovel silence in turns
    Like filling a grave with dirt
Filling a grave with peace
We buoy each other with close by knees
    Close by knees and hearts in a row
    There is no space between the warmth

Space fills with our particulars

While time wears off the edges

    Cushions and nests don't have edges

    We never let our fledglings fall

Falling back and letting go

Our private efforts, common goals

    Each private inhale smells incense

    A twist of smoke draws a squint from us all

ADVICE IN A LOCUST SWARM

During the pandemic
my Aunt Joan visits in a dream
with two sister oracles
floating by her side
in the sky
A locust swarm descends
upon me and a tree
The self-writhing mass
of the insects
with clacking clothespin
shape and color and sound
dims the light
They hit my body all over
with small thumps
I am carefully extracting
half a locust
from my right ear
and gesturing I'm Ok
I'm fine with my left hand
when my aunt
speaks from above
the noise and says

Slow down
Don't run in a locust swarm
I take her advice
and walk a path
It helps so much
that later I can recall
that every process
simply responds and turns
in its time
The wave gathers and shatters
The body switches to inhale
The swarm dips and reforms

THISTLE

An afternoon
when the wind carried
pure hot sorrow
it plucked thistle puff seeds
from a dry batch
and sent them off
in ones or twos or fives
in their delicate radial curtsy
to asphalt or vast sky
or hoods of cars
or who knows where
Seeing them tumble humbly forward
in their light and symmetrical grace
holding hands or solo
no orientation
no destination
all reach and no bearing
I feel the truth of loss and lost
and the salvation of my role
as blank witness

"...WITHOUT ANY HINDRANCE, NO FEARS EXIST."

from *The Maha Prajna Paramita Hridaya Sutra*

All streams have rocks
All riverbeds, silt
Water is clarity
Intimate with gravity

White butterflies never
Fly a straight line
Their course shows the progress
Of distractability

The blind beating heart
Pumping blue branches
If exposed to oxygen's magic
Expels bright red pools

TETRALEMMA IV

dilemma split
trilemma crack
tetralemma table
pentalemma progress

THE BACK-POEM

Behind every line, the one left on the road
(every variation of all not said)
Sculpted air rings with word shape
(how silence feels the same coming into or out of the ear)
The direction the lines pull
(the swerving searching eyes when the child vanishes)
The gently encasing sense of meaning
(reference points ditch you and duck out)
Follow the flow with hope or not
(or drop)
You ask questions like Where? and What color is her t-shirt?
(a child's cry contains every sound like white light contains every color)
It's not just the moving pieces in the story
(it's the moving stories in the pieces)
Flip a switch; the outcome filters feelings
(what remains in the raw guts post-exhale)
An empty interior awaits
(an empty awaiting creates)

ACKNOWLEDGEMENTS

I am deeply grateful to all Buddhas and ancestors who cleared paths so I could clear paths to poems. This includes Roshi Sojun Diane Martin who opened this process, and Neal Gordon, Perie Longo and Alma Rolfs who attended it with such heart. I am also deeply grateful to my loving friends, sangha, the 'Perennials,' and the children of Family Focus who give me grace and joy.

Especially and eternally, I thank my family, Clay, Tara, Rick and the gray cat Zane.

PUBLICATION ACKNOWLEDGEMENTS

"Dust Collects Shadows" originally published in *The Journal of Poetry Therapy*, 23:3, August 2010, reprinted with permission.

"How Change Happens, Air Carries and Thistle" originally published in *The Journal of Poetry Therapy*, 33:1, November 2019, reprinted with permission.

"Thistle" also published in *Beyond Words* September 2020, reprinted with permission.

"A Spring Day in the Pandemic, Pandemic Journal" and "Advice in a Locust Swarm" originally published in *The Museletter* of the National Association of Poetry Therapy; July 2020, reprinted with permission.

ABOUT THE AUTHOR

Beth Jacobs is a writer, clinical psychologist and transmitted lay teacher in the Soto Zen tradition. She is the author of *Writing for Emotional Balance, Paper Sky, The Original Buddhist Psychology,* and *A Buddhist Journal,* and she facilitates expressive writing groups with children and grandparents. She lives with her beloved family and gray cat. Her work serves to encourage the unique enlightened voice within each being.

HOMEBOUND
PUBLICATIONS

We are an award-winning independent publisher founded in 2011 striving to ensure that the mainstream is not the only stream. More than a company, we are a community of writers and readers exploring the larger questions we face as a global village. It is our intention to preserve contemplative storytelling. We publish full-length introspective works of creative non-fiction, literary fiction, and poetry. *Fly with us into our 10th year.*

WWW.HOMEBOUNDPUBLICATIONS.COM

CPSIA information can be obtained
at www.ICGtesting.com
Printed in the USA
JSHW040031070421
13335JS00001B/39